The Art Of Feeling

POEMS For Those Who Feel And Those Who Cannot Feel.

LEAH "LARRABEE" PALM

To order additional copies of this book, contact:
Xlibris
844-714-8691
www.Xlibris.com
Orders@Xlibris.com

ISBN: Softcover   979-8-3694-4388-0
         Hardcover   979-8-3694-4389-7
         EBook   979-8-3694-4380-4

Library of Congress Control Number: 2025906954

Print information available on the last page

Rev. date: 05/02/2025

Christine stated, "that the poems were moving, and she particularly liked the two poems entitled "Now" and "How do you say goodbye to a butterfly".

-CHRISTINE POWERS
Executive Director, Brookdale Senior Living

"Dear LEAH "LARRABEE" PALM,
Oh this book of poems! Every single one that I read, touched on my life, my soul and touched on the remembrance and feelings of those they reminded me of. Thank you from the bottom of my heart for assembling this collection."

-KRISTIE MOON
Sales Marketing Director, Brookdale Senior Living

"If you need someone to help you, you need look no further. For Leah is loving of heart and mind. She is also gentle of soul. Her book reflects her. She is generous of nature and is a people person. I am proud to call her my friend and honored to have my poem in her book."

-NELLIE
Retired School Teacher
Resident, Brookdale Senior Living

Reading these poems opened my eyes to things I might not have considered before. The depth of the emotions and words combine for holistic approach to poetry. Her experience in the Army and care for patients and friends shines.

-WILL RAVENSTEIN
Assoc. Pastor
Junction City First United Methodist Church

This book is dedicated to VBS.

Contents

Foreword

Poems can be short and concise, or lengthy and verbose.
One thing they will surely do, is to help you emote your feelings.
So, I hope when you read these poems in this book, that you
experience feelings of some kind. If they do this for you,
then I have accomplished what I intended when writing this book.

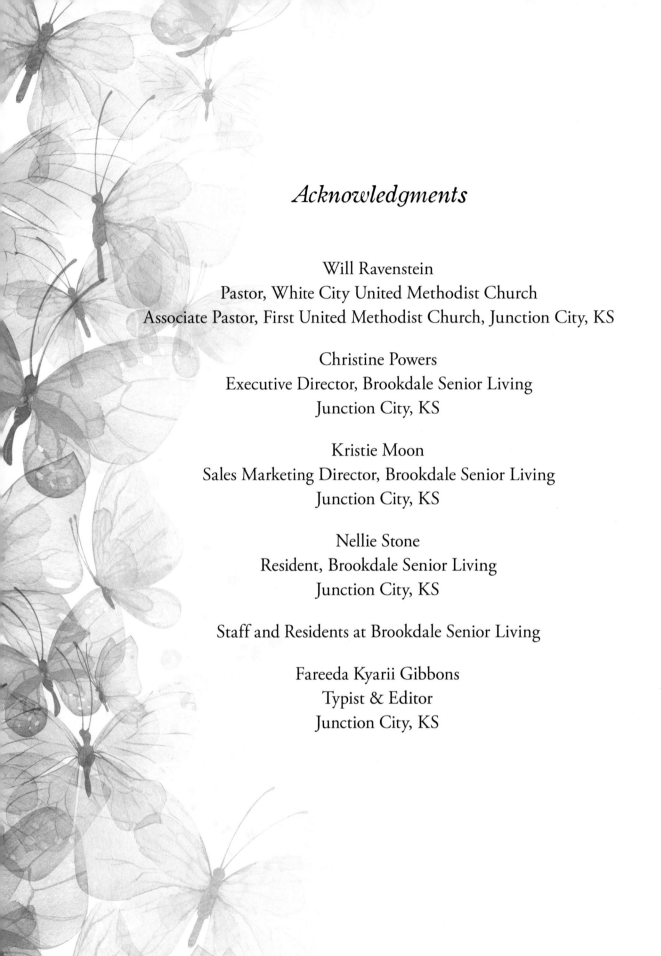

Acknowledgments

Will Ravenstein
Pastor, White City United Methodist Church
Associate Pastor, First United Methodist Church, Junction City, KS

Christine Powers
Executive Director, Brookdale Senior Living
Junction City, KS

Kristie Moon
Sales Marketing Director, Brookdale Senior Living
Junction City, KS

Nellie Stone
Resident, Brookdale Senior Living
Junction City, KS

Staff and Residents at Brookdale Senior Living

Fareeda Kyarii Gibbons
Typist & Editor
Junction City, KS

The Art Of Feeling

POEMS For Those Who Feel And Those Who Cannot Feel.

LEAH "LARRABEE" PALM

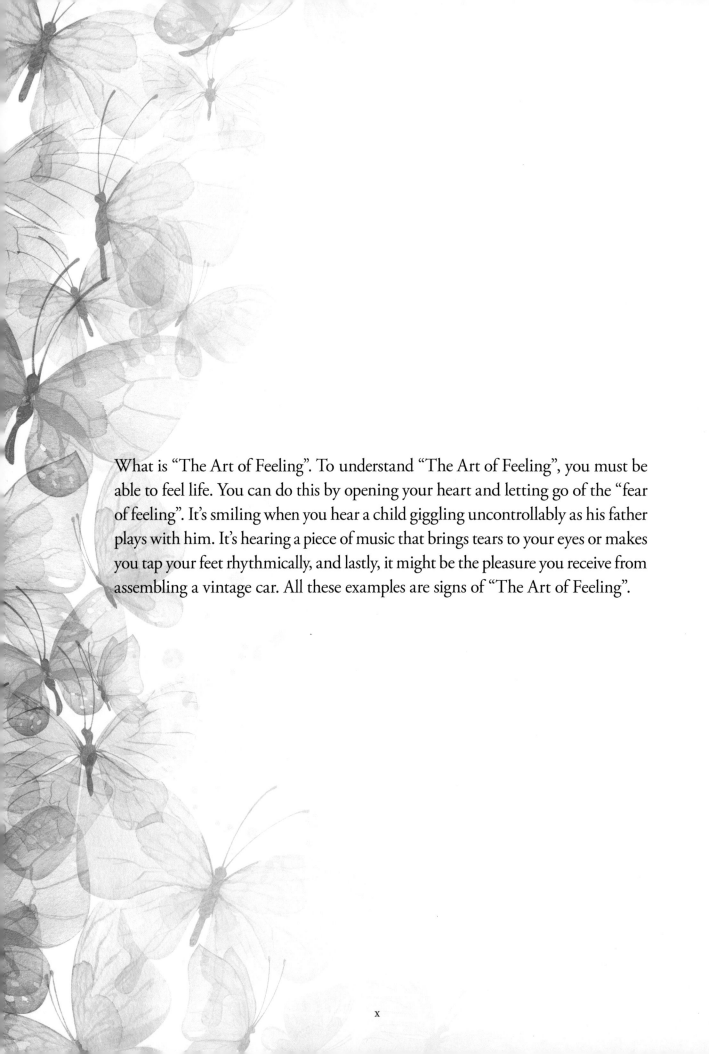

What is "The Art of Feeling". To understand "The Art of Feeling", you must be able to feel life. You can do this by opening your heart and letting go of the "fear of feeling". It's smiling when you hear a child giggling uncontrollably as his father plays with him. It's hearing a piece of music that brings tears to your eyes or makes you tap your feet rhythmically, and lastly, it might be the pleasure you receive from assembling a vintage car. All these examples are signs of "The Art of Feeling".

MODIFIED MONOPOLY

Nellie is a 97 year-old retired schoolteacher of thirty-plus years, and a mother of two sons. Over the years she has slowly lost her vision and hearing.

She does not allow the loss of these two senses to define her. This is true because she is also a courageous and intelligent person. When it comes to learning new experiences, such as playing monopoly, she becomes excited and motivated.

So, when a friend asked her if she would like to play monopoly, Nellie said, "I will try, but I don't see how I can play." Thus began the saga of Nellie and monopoly. Soon it was obvious that Nellie was thoroughly enthralled with the game.

Nellie began to want to play more and more and more; even when she was tired. Her friends began to think that Nellie had "fallen in love" with the game of monopoly. This seemed so because she continued to play monopoly to this day and she is circa 98 years old.

THE ANGEL ROOM

Angels of various character and origin
Hang from the ceiling and rest
Lightly against the walls.

Water trickles over the dark and uneven
Surface of a miniature waterfall.

Beside the waterfall is seated a gentle-faced
Buddha. She is adorned with a symbol for longevity.

Music, barely perceptible to the human ear,
Fills the seven-by-nine-foot room.

A painted and framed outdoor scene
Is attached to the back wall.

Particles of aromatic elixirs float
From a dark corner of the small room.

The room is dimly lit. You can see the
Shadow of a person moving within it.

Seen also are the shapes of a table,
A chair, and a plinth. Yet somehow
These forms merge into nothingness.

It is as though both the animate and
Inanimate have integrated
Their elements into one existence.

It is a world apart, this room,
This room called "The Angel's Room."

HOW DO YOU SAY GOODBYE TO A BUTTERFLY

There is a full moon shining into my bedroom tonight; and
I ponder, "How do you say goodbye to a butterfly?"

There are mid-day moons in Russia, as there are in the USA.
However, the fullness curves to the left instead of to the right; So, I
wonder, which is the better way to say, "goodbye to a Butterfly?"

In China, I see a blistering sunburst with an extended, falling tail,
that stretches from the top of the mountain to the surface below.

And I ask myself, how does one safely ascend such
a height to say; "goodbye to a butterfly?"

In Texas, there are great plains, over which I will travel
alone. So, I must ask, will what I have now, grow, and
if not, how do I say, "goodbye to a butterfly?"

Ah, the answer is so simple that one cannot see the "how."
For only the acceptance of truth provides the strength
and courage to say, "goodbye to a butterfly."

I THINK OF YOU

When I laugh hilariously during a play
I think of you.

When I walk alone in my cul-de-sac
I think of you.

When I see a person astride a horse
I think of you.

When I gaze at an empty chair in a restaurant
I think of you.

When I drive a distance in my car
I think of you.

When I reach for your hand, and it is not there
I think of you.

When I hear a song and wish to dance
I think of you.

When I play my thumb drum each night
I think of you.

After more than three years of thinking of you
I still think of you.

MID-DAY MOON

You are my mid-day moon.

Unexpectedly, you appear in the soft-blue sky,

Between the top branches of two trees

That reach over and across the road

Trying to touch their leaves.

My car travels beneath the branches as

I avert my eyes and peer through the patchwork of limbs

Trying not to lose sight of your hazy, opaque, sphere

As the shape of you fades away and dims.

Too quickly my car passes under you, to go on its way

And I can see you no more.

The day has darkened, and you are gone

And no matter how much I implore,

You must go, for you are truly a night-time moon

That must disappear from my daytime, very soon.

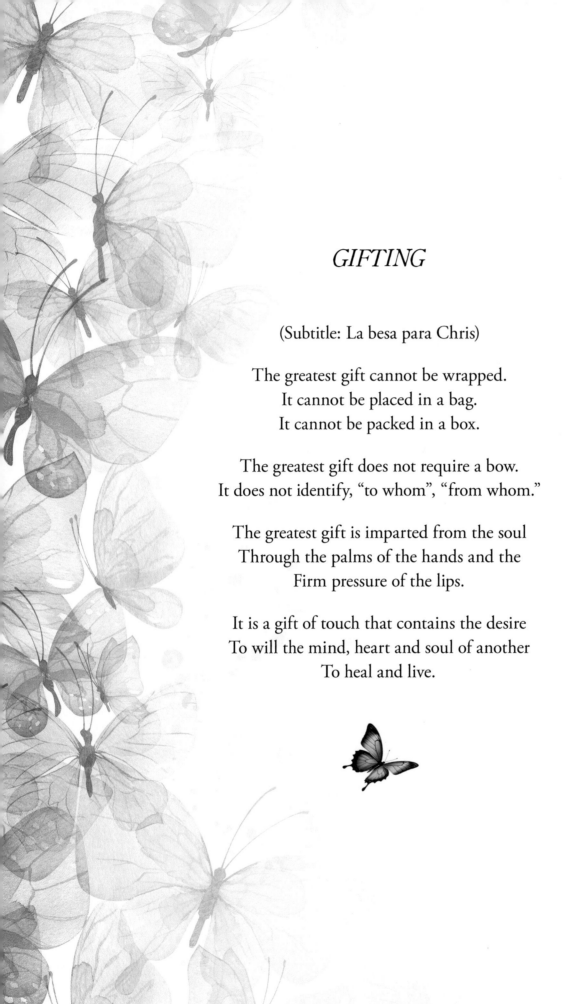

GIFTING

(Subtitle: La besa para Chris)

The greatest gift cannot be wrapped.
It cannot be placed in a bag.
It cannot be packed in a box.

The greatest gift does not require a bow.
It does not identify, "to whom", "from whom."

The greatest gift is imparted from the soul
Through the palms of the hands and the
Firm pressure of the lips.

It is a gift of touch that contains the desire
To will the mind, heart and soul of another
To heal and live.

WHO ARE YOU?

Who are you?
You are someone outside yourself.

You are more than yourself.
You are one with your universe.

You have quick and accurate insights.
They reach beyond your years.

Your presence occupies a room as
An actor fills her stage.

Time has neither boundaries nor
Limitations for you.
You float gently through it.

You inhale the air of life as does
A winded horse; with nostrils flaring.

No one I have known the world
Over, is similar to you.

So "Who are you?" you are a mystery.
You are new to me.

LADY IN BLACK

Sunlight, sunlight
What a delight
It fills me with warmth
To see such a sight.

It is the creation of brilliance
Burning through and through
It is so very bright
It seems brand new

It is the mirror of truth
That reflects such youth
It is the result of "turning and turning"
And "coming out right."

Sunlight, sunlight
What a delight.
It fills me with warmth
To see such a sight.

YOU ARE SO EASY TO LOVE

You are so easy to love
When your voice soothes my thoughts
With words that quiet my soul.

You are so easy to love
When your hand strokes away my pain,
And your spirit touches my heart.

You are so easy to love, so easy to trust,
And I admit, I do love you, for at this time,
I must.

NOW

A couple weeks ago you whispered; almost to yourself

That you were running out of time.

Yet we all have the same amount of time.

Only "now."

We have neither the moment before "now"

Nor the moment after "now."

Only "now."

So, know you are not running out of time

For you are living, very much so, in the "now."

THE COURAGEOUS SOUL

The courageous soul is one that is wise and kind.

It is a soul that has suffered, given and forgiven.

The courageous soul is as sweet as nectar.

It is a soul that has loved and been loved.

It is a confident soul; a rare soul; a courageous soul.

INSIGHTS AFTER SIXTY-FIVE

I feel so alone and so vulnerable at this age.
I cannot think of what to do or how to begin it.

Yet I must live on and create a second life:
Short through it may seem.

Amazingly, the second life begins as did the first;
Lovingly, hopefully, sadly.

However now, courage must be sought after;
For it no longer occurs spontaneously.

Conscious effort of thought must override
The feeling of inertia.

And I must delve deep inside me to make
A friend of confidence.

My belief and trust in an unpredictable, body
And mind, must be met with comfort.

All this has to be accomplished in order that
I might continue to live a life filled with
Opportunity and humor

"After----sixty-five."

Dedicated to Florence M. Uecker
July 6, 1926 – July 28, 2005

LEE CORPORAN

From out of no where arose Lee Corporan;
A five-foot six, fifty-five-year-old woman who
Was adrift and struggling her way through life.

She was someone whom initially, I would
Not have chosen for a friend.

Yet, there was something about her
That piqued my curiosity.

So, thanks to her persistent nature,
I slowly began to know her genuine side.
Then I began to trust her.

I started to understand her anxious side.
The side that two head tumors and
A heart disability played in her life.

I learned the side of her that had earned
three years of college; the side that was a mother,
A grandmother: the side that craved love
And friendship; the side that was spiritual.
The side that was responsible and lastly,
The side that wanted to begin life anew.

THE CAROUSEL OF MANIA

Do not call me.
I wish to remain alone in my melancholy.
Do not try to encourage or mobilize me.
The effort will be futile and often unwelcome.

For the problem I have is intrinsic.
It makes me irritable.
It is not transitory.
It is permanent.

It is not curable.
It is cyclical.
It mimics a chameleon; it changes often.
It is a teaser and a troublemaker.

I feel good; I feel friendly.
Life is nice; I buy things.
My debts grow.

I speak out harshly.
My friends bid farewell.

Round and round and up and down I go,
Much like a horse on a carousel.

TORNADO

My life mimics a tornado.

Clear one moment; cloudy the next.

Throwing me here; tossing me there.

Touching down; rising high.

Calm as can be.

Yet permanently; a calamity.

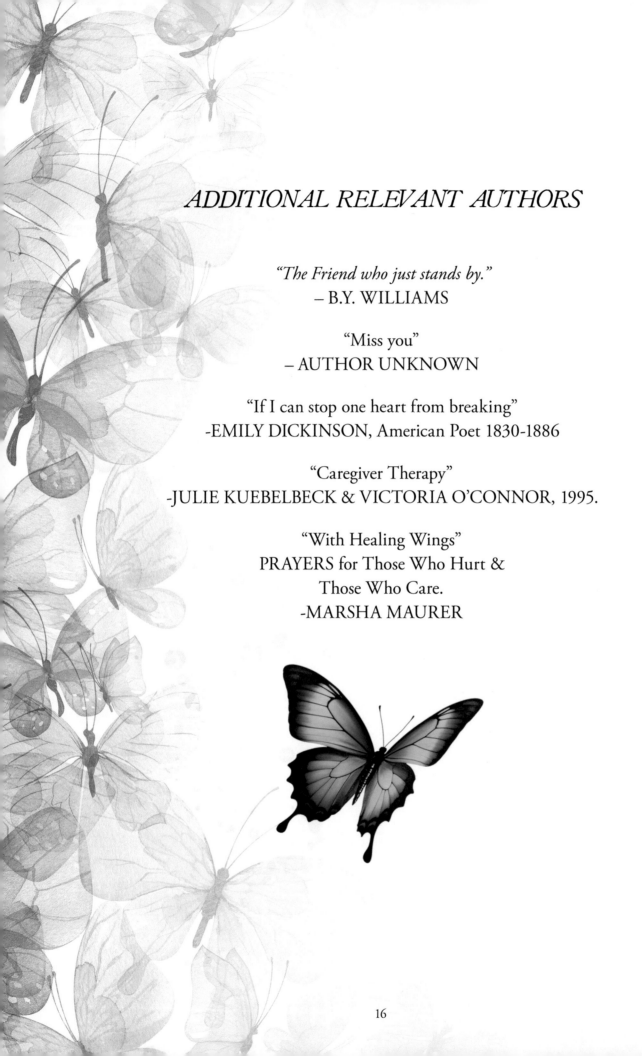

ADDITIONAL RELEVANT AUTHORS

"The Friend who just stands by."
– B.Y. WILLIAMS

"Miss you"
– AUTHOR UNKNOWN

"If I can stop one heart from breaking"
-EMILY DICKINSON, American Poet 1830-1886

"Caregiver Therapy"
-JULIE KUEBELBECK & VICTORIA O'CONNOR, 1995.

"With Healing Wings"
PRAYERS for Those Who Hurt &
Those Who Care.
-MARSHA MAURER

"THE FRIEND WHO JUST STANDS BY"

When trouble comes your soul to try,
You love the friend who just "stands by."

Perhaps there's nothing he can do —
The thing is strictly up to you;

For there are troubles all your own,
And paths the soul must tread alone;

Time when love cannot smooth the road
Nor friendship lift the heavy load,

But just to know you have a friend
Who will "stand by" until the end,

Whose sympathy through all endures,
Whose warm handclasp is always yours —

It helps, someway, to pull you through,
Although there's nothing he can do.

And so with fervent heart you cry,
"God bless the friend who just 'stands by'!"

- B.Y. Williams

"MISS YOU"

I miss you in the morning, dear,
    —When all the world is new;
I know the day can bring no joy
    —Because it brings not you.
I miss the well-loved voice of you,
    —Your tender smile for me,
The charm of you, the joy of your
    —Unfailing sympathy.

The world is full of folks, it's true,
    —But there was only one of you.

I miss you at the noontide, dear;
    The crowded city street
Seems but a desert now, I walk
    —In solitude complete.
I miss your hand beside my own
    —The light touch of your hand,
The quick gleam in the eyes of you
    —So sure to understand.

The world is full of folks, it's true,
    —But there was only one of you.

I miss you in the evening, dear,
    —When daylight fades away;
I miss the sheltering arms of you
    —To rest me from the day,
I try to think I see you yet
—There were the firefight gleams—
Weary at last, I sleep, and still
    —I miss you in my dreams.

"IF I CAN STOP ONE HEART FROM BREAKING"

If I can stop one heart from breaking, I shall not live in vain.
If I can ease one life the aching, or cool one pain,
Or help one lonely person into happiness again,
I shall not live in vain.
-Emily Dickinson-

"CAREGIVER THERAPY"

Living fully includes caring for yourself, and
Giving care to others. Keeping both in balance
Will make your journey through life
Rich and rewarding.
-Julie Kuebelbeck & Victoria O'Connor-

"WITH HEALING WINGS"
As Aging
(A Prayer)

Lord of Hope,

I hoped to live long, yet I am surprised to grow old so quickly. As my years accumulate, I struggle with the challenges of declining energy and strength, of slower limbs and wits, of precarious health. Yet despite diminished faculty and facility, I praise You that I retain with assurance, I can face the limits of impairment and dependence, the loss of dear ones, the disturbance of change. Give me purpose, bravery, enthusiasm, and cheer. Assuage my frustration and forgive my complaint. Make me patient in adversity, positive in attitude, persistent in hope. May I never abandon my effort, but incline always onward, upward and nearer to You. Amen.

-Marsha Maurer-

IMAGE ATTRIBUTIONS

Butterflies
-Image by jemastock on Freepik.

Cover Photo
-Image by storyset on Freepik.

THE END

Printed in the United States
by Baker & Taylor Publisher Services